The English Colonization of America

EXPLORATION AND DISCOVERY

EXPLORATION AND DISCOVERY

The English Colonization of America

How explorers and colonists such as
Sir Walter Raleigh, John Smith, and
Miles Standish helped establish England's
presence in the New World

Dan Harvey

Mason Crest Publishers
Philadelphia

Mason Crest Publishers
370 Reed Road
Broomall PA 19008

Copyright © 2003 by Mason Crest Publishers. All rights
reserved. Printed and bound in the Hashemite Kingdom of
Jordan

First printing

1 3 5 7 9 8 6 4 2

Library of Congress Cataloging-in-Publication Data
on file at the Library of Congress

ISBN 1-59084-051-8

 EXPLORATION **AND DISCOVERY**

Contents

This 1587 map of the American coastline from Virginia to Florida was drawn by John White. To the right of the crest at the upper right, several ships sail near a string of islands. One of these islands was Roanoke Island, the site of an early English settlement in North America.

What Happened on Roanoke Island?

WHEN JOHN White came ashore at Roanoke Island in the summer of 1590, he must have known something was terribly wrong.

Three years earlier, White had said good-bye to a group of colonists on this same sandy shore. He had left them with a promise to return. As his ship sailed into the harbor near the settlement he had left, White thought he saw a signal fire. However, when White stepped on the island, no one came to greet him. Where had everyone gone?

Hoping to find answers, White began exploring the small, *barrier reef* island, which is located off the eastern coast of North America in the present-day state of North

Carolina. Because of the plentiful vegetation and abundant wildlife, many of White's countrymen and fellow explorers had called this New World a paradise. But White, who had first come to the island five years earlier as part of a group sponsored by the English nobleman Sir Walter Raleigh, understood that this unexplored continent was an untamed and dangerous land. The weather was often harsh, and the native people could be unpredictable. Gazing about, White must have felt that his worst fears had come true.

Raleigh had tried to establish a colony in 1585, but it didn't last. White, a noted explorer and *cartographer*, or mapmaker, had returned in 1587 to try again. More than 100 *emigrants*—including men, women, and children— had sailed with him down the Thames River in England to the Atlantic Ocean and then across the sea, determined to establish a colony in the New World.

White would be the governor of the settlement. He seemed a good choice for leader. By July of that year, the colony appeared to be healthy, and it looked as though England had established its first settlement in North America. A child had even been born in August to John White's daughter Eleanor and her husband Annanias Dare. The child's name was Virginia Dare, and she was the first English child born in North America.

But where was John White's granddaughter now?

John White

John White was one of England's first explorers of North America. His skills as an artist and mapmaker were just as important as his accomplishments as an explorer and colonist. Wherever he went, he used watercolor paints to make pictures of the people, places, and things that he saw.

White's artwork proved to be an important source of information. Other explorers studied his paintings, many of which were reproduced in books. Some were included in *A Briefe and True Report of the New Found Land of Virginia*, an important book written by Thomas Hariot.

White went on several notable voyages with other well-known explorers. In 1577, he sailed with Martin Frobisher in search of gold and the northwest passage to Asia. During that voyage, he visited Greenland. In 1585, he sailed under the charter that had been issued to Sir Walter Raleigh to explore and colonize Roanoke Island.

When White retired to Ireland in 1593, he wrote a book about his last trip to Virginia and Roanoke Island.

Almost immediately after the colonists had arrived in 1587, White had to sail back to England to get more supplies. He promised he would return as soon as he could. He did not like the idea of leaving, but the return voyage was

What does the name "Roanoke" mean? Actually, two meanings have been applied. It is a Native American term that means "northern people," and it also stands for a "place where shell beads are found."

necessary for the survival of the colony. As he departed, White had no way of knowing it would be the last time he would see his family.

While White was gone, the colonists no doubt endured harsh weather conditions. Roanoke and other nearby islands are subjected to strong winds, and the shores are pounded by rough surf. Often, the coast of that part of the continent is beset by *hurricanes*.

Still, the land was rich with resources, and it appeared to be a place that could sustain life. Indeed, tribes of native people thrived in the area. The Croatoans were described as tall and strong. For the most part, they were friendly to the English newcomers.

There was much to fear, however, from other Native Americans in the area. During the first attempt to settle Roanoke in 1585, there had been trouble between the colonists and an unfriendly tribe. In fact, because of these problems the new colonists did not want to start their settlement on Roanoke Island. Instead, they wanted to establish the new colony somewhere to the north, in the Chesapeake Bay area. The Portuguese sailor who piloted their ship, however, wanted to return to Europe as soon as he could and dropped them off on Roanoke.

Back in England, White was unable to make a quick return. His country was preparing for war with Spain. All ships would be needed to help fight off the Spanish *armada*, so English supply ships could not sail to North America. White was forced to remain in England for three years while England and Spain fought. Each and every day, he must have worried about the colonists and the family members he had left behind—especially his granddaughter. Finally, in 1590, after England had defeated Spain, John White was able to return to Roanoke Island.

White arrived on August 18, 1590. Virginia Dare would have been three years old on that day. Now, as White continued exploring the island on his granddaughter's birthday, he came upon some sights that surely must have made his heart sink. At the deserted settlement, the settlers had built *fortifications*. Had they been expecting some kind of attack?

White found few clues to the colonists' fate. Someone had carved the letters "CRO" into the bark of a tree and "Croatoan" into the colony's wooden fortifications. What were the meanings of these crude inscriptions? Did the colonists go off to live with the Indians, as some believed? Or did the words have a darker meaning? Did the carvings mean that the Croatoan Indians had attacked the colony?

The fate of the Roanoke Island colony remains a mystery. The colonists may have become absorbed into a local Native American tribe, or they may have been wiped out by hostile Indians.

White believed the colonists went to live with the Croatoans. However, when he tried to find out for sure, he was hit with more bad luck. His explorations were cut short by a hurricane. His ships were damaged, and he was forced to return to England.

Back in England, he tried several times to raise money for another return voyage. He was unsuccessful. John White would never return to Roanoke Island.

To this day, no one really knows what happened to the "lost colony" of Roanoke Island, although there are plenty of theories. Some believe that the settlers traveled south to Croatoan Island to live with the Indians, and eventually became part of the Croatoan tribe. Others believe that the colonists split into groups, with some members going to the Chesapeake Bay area.

The Roanoke experience was not a good start for the English colonization of North America. Efforts to colonize the New World would be put on hold for more than 15 years. Other settlers would eventually follow, however, and they would establish successful colonies in North America.

The Roanoke experience demonstrated the risks of attempting to settle in a land full of hostile conditions. Those who came later endured the same hardships as the Roanoke colonists: hunger, disease, conflict with the natives, and harsh weather. Yet they survived. And their hard work gave rise to the 13 English colonies, the concept of self-government, and, ultimately, the birth of the United States of America.

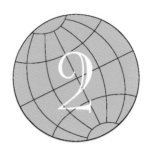

The Early Explorers

THOUGH THE voyages of Christopher Columbus opened the door for the great European Age of Exploration, and, ultimately, to the colonization of North America, many now accept that it was not Columbus who discovered America. The Vikings, who lived in the Scandinavian countries of Norway, Sweden, Denmark, and Finland, were among the first Europeans who reached these shores. Archeological evidence suggests that Leif Eriksson landed on the northern part of the North American continent about a thousand years ago. However, Columbus's voyages, made between 1492 and 1502, inspired other Europeans and ultimately led to the colonization of the continent.

The English Colonization of North America

Of course, people already lived in the New World long before Europeans established any colonies there. The original inhabitants of North America are thought to have migrated from Asia around 50,000 B.C., crossing the Bering Strait to reach the huge continent.

As more people came to North America, people spread south and east across the land. These primitive people were hunters and gatherers, who used crude tools and weapons. (Their prey even included the huge wooly mammoth.) These people were believed to be the earliest ancestors of the Native Americans who inhabited the continent when the Europeans first arrived.

During the 16th century, many of these Europeans were Spanish soldiers and explorers. However, Spain focused on exploring and conquering native populations in South America, Central America, and the southern part of North America. In the early part of the 16th century, explorers such as Juan Ponce de León, Hernan Cortés, Vasco Núñez de Balboa, Francisco Pizarro, and Hernando de Soto landed in such locations as Florida, Mexico, Panama, and Peru.

The Spanish explorers, unlike the later English explorers, were conquerors intent on finding gold and forcibly converting the native people to Christianity. They saw the New World as a source of riches and exploited the land and its people.

While the Spaniards were exploring the southwestern regions of North America, France was establishing settlements in what are now Canada and the northern part of the United States. Notable explorers who claimed land for France included Jacques Cartier, who explored the Gulf of Saint Lawrence and the area that would one day become the city of Montreal, and Samuel de Champlain, who founded Quebec. In these northern climates, the French established fur-trading posts.

At the start of the European age of exploration, England didn't make as many voyages as other countries. One of the first notable English voyages took place in 1497, when John Cabot, an Italian navigator sailing in the service of the English king, Henry VII, explored the northern coast of North America. Cabot tried to find a *northwest passage* to Asia, a goal shared by many early explorers. Cabot did not find the passage, but, because of his voyage, England laid claim to the North American continent.

However, England did not have much interest in acting upon this claim at this time. The country had little money, so it made no effort to establish any colonies. England's next

> **John Cabot was paid only £10—roughly the equivalent of $10—for his 1497 voyage to North America. He made a second voyage in 1498, but never returned.**

The Unsuccessful Explorers

A number of Englishmen explored North America during the 16th and early 17th centuries. Most were searching for a route to Asia—the northwest passage. In 1576 Sir Humphrey Gilbert (pictured) claimed that a water route led around North America to Asia. A few years later Gilbert sailed to Newfoundland, where he wanted to start a colony from which he could search for the northwest passage. However, the colony failed, and Gilbert died when his ship sank.

Two other English captains, Martin Frobisher and John Davis, each made three voyages between 1575 and 1589. They explored the waterways north of the St. Lawrence River, in modern-day Canada, but neither could find a way to the Pacific.

During the early years of the 17th century, Henry Hudson made four voyages of exploration—three of them for England. However, Hudson is most famous for a voyage he made under the Dutch flag. During that 1609 voyage, he followed a waterway into North America and claimed land for Holland. The river today bears his name, the Hudson River, and the land he claimed would become a Dutch colony, later renamed New York.

ruler, the notorious King Henry VIII, was too busy with problems at home to spend time planning the colonization of North America.

England finally began exploring in earnest at the end of the 16th century. Some English sailors were still driven by the belief that it was possible to sail around the New World and reach Asia if they could find the northwest passage. Others thought that English exploration would help stop expansion by Spain, England's rival.

One notable early English explorer was Martin Frobisher. He tried three times to find the northwest passage. Another English explorer, Sir Francis Drake, sailed around the world between 1577 and 1580.

Sir Humphrey Gilbert, a soldier and sailor, was one of the first Englishmen who tried to establish permanent colonies in the New World. In 1583, Gilbert sailed to Newfoundland, where he hoped to create an English colony. However, the settlement lasted less than a year before the settlers returned to England. In September of that year, while sailing the treacherous waters of the North Atlantic, Gilbert was lost at sea with five ships and 260 men.

Sir Walter Raleigh, an English nobleman who was a popular member of Queen Elizabeth's court, was the next to try to establish permanent colonies. He received a *charter* from the queen, giving him permission to create a settlement in a large area Raleigh called Virginia.

Although Raleigh himself never explored or lived in North America, he sent out four expeditions between 1584 and 1590. The first landed at Roanoke Island and looked for sites for a possible settlement. The second, in 1585, was involved in an initial colonization attempt that failed. After a year, the colonists returned to England. The more than 100 people who took part in the third expedition, in 1587, disappeared from Roanoke Island. The fourth expedition amounted to little more than an unsuccessful search for the colonists.

When they landed, the English usually encountered woodland Indians, who inhabited the eastern part of North America. These natives lived in an area between the Chesapeake Bay and South Carolina. Like their ancestors, they hunted, fished, and grew their own crops. They lived in organized societies, or tribes, with leaders and priests.

The land supplied the woodland Indians with much of their food. The men of the tribes hunted for small game, including duck, geese, turkey, squirrels, rabbits, and raccoons. They also hunted deer. They not only got food from deer, but they got their clothing as well. The nearby ocean provided fish and shellfish. The Indians were also good farmers. They knew a lot about agriculture and they lived in

Sir Walter Raleigh

Although Sir Walter Raleigh had many adventures, and also made smoking tobacco popular, he may be best known for a famous chivalric gesture. Raleigh reportedly laid his cloak over a puddle for Queen Elizabeth to step across. This was a gesture typical of Raleigh. He was described as dashing, charming, brave, and handsome, and he was a favorite of the queen.

Raleigh was born in 1552 near Devon, England. During his active life, he was a explorer, soldier, and even a pirate. His explorations with Sir Humphrey Gilbert, his half brother, helped open the door to English colonization. He was also a scholar and writer.

During his life, many people viewed Raleigh as a hero. Others thought of him as a scoundrel. Queen Elizabeth's successor, King James I, even accused Raleigh of treason. The accusation turned out to be false, but Raleigh was imprisoned for a long time. He was finally executed on October 29, 1618, by being beheaded. It was said that he went to his death in much the same way that he lived his life: with courage and style. He reportedly joked with his executioner before the ax finally fell.

> **Corn was an important food item to the woodland Indians—possibly the most important one. They used it to make bread and pancakes and they used it in a stew that consisted of fish and other vegetables.**

a fertile area. Their crops included corn, beans, squash, and pumpkins.

These native people were there to meet the English as they arrived in North America. Despite the early failures at colonization, in the early years of the 17th century England restarted its exploration of the New World. There were several reasons for this. England's naval power had grown considerably, so it could establish and protect settlements far from the home country. Also, English businessmen saw an opportunity to make money by bringing raw materials from other countries to England, where they could be sold at a profit. They also wanted to sell finished goods to countries outside of Europe. These businessmen set up private trading companies, which paid for England's explorations and colonization attempts. Such companies included the Muscovy Company, which was formed to trade with Russia, and the London Company.

These companies had no problem finding men to lead these explorations. England was experiencing its Renaissance period, and many of the era's Renaissance men sought adventure. Renaissance men were adventurous, courageous individuals who were well educated and well traveled. A typical Renaissance man was a scholar, soldier, and professional adventurer.

In 1606, after the failures on Roanoke Island, the London Company (renamed the Virginia Company) began making plans for a colony in Jamestown. King James I granted the company a charter. Soon, settlers would set out for North America, to start what would become England's first successful colony.

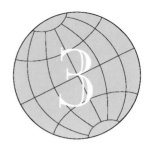

Jamestown

IMAGINE WHAT it must have been like to be a settler. As you stand on the London docks, ready to depart, you realize you are leaving everything behind: friends, family, home, and country. The enormous Atlantic Ocean will present an wide *chasm* between your old life and new life. The sea voyage will be cramped, cold, and uncomfortable, and it will last two or three months. When you reach the shore, there will be no comfortable place where you can rest your weary body. If you want shelter, you will have to build it.

When you first land on shore, the New World appears a strange and dangerous place. It is filled with wild animals and unusual plants and it is inhabited by a strange people.

They look different, speak a different language, and could very well be hostile. What if they don't want you here?

That is how the early settlers must have felt as they prepared to leave England for Virginia.

The English colony of Jamestown—England's first successful colony in North America—was named after King James I, the British ruler at the time the settlement was established. Today, however, we associate one name above all with Jamestown: Captain John Smith. Under Smith's leadership, the colonists overcame severe hardships and trials to create the first permanent English settlement in North America.

Like many notable figures in the history of English exploration and colonization, Smith gained a reputation as a rugged, unique individual. Like Sir Walter Raleigh, Smith was a well-traveled adventurer and soldier. He stood on the docks of a London port on the morning of December 20, 1606, waiting to set sail with 105 other men. The Virginia Company had invested in three ships that would take these men to America. Their instructions: establish a colony in Virginia.

The group included English gentlemen, *artisans*, craftsmen, and laborers. At the time, these men didn't think of Smith as any kind of leader. Many felt he was an overbearing, swaggering braggart and liar. At sea, Smith had trouble

King James I of England, who had succeeded Queen Elizabeth in 1603, encouraged exploration. In 1606 he granted a charter to the Virginia Company to establish what would become the first permanent English settlement, Jamestown. King James also sponsored such explorers of North America as Henry Hudson and Walter Raleigh. When Raleigh failed in his mission to find gold in South America, the king had him beheaded for treason.

getting along with some of the men. In fact, when the settlers reached America, Smith was below deck in chains. Attitudes about Smith, however, would eventually change. It was his presence that made the difference during the colony's first and hardest years.

The colonists arrived at Virginia on May 14, 1607. The ships landed on the banks of the James River (also named after the king) 60 miles south of Chesapeake Bay. On shore, the men went right to work building shelters, a storehouse, and a church.

One of the first things Smith did was search for the lost colonists of Roanoke. He found evidence that they had been in the area. Smith learned from the local Algonquin Indians that some of the colonists had gone to live with a

The English come ashore at Jamestown (top) and begin building their settlement (opposite) in the spring of 1607.

friendly tribe in the Chesapeake Bay region. But Smith also was told that a local Indian chief, Powhatan, had attacked the colonists and killed most of them.

Almost from the start, things started going bad for the colony. The environment proved harsh; the settlers found they lacked adequate supplies; and some of the men didn't like the idea of hard work. They were "gentlemen," who felt they were too good to do physical labor. The settlers had trouble with the local Indians, too. To protect themselves from the Algonquians, they had to erect a triangular fort around the other structures they had built. Crop failure, disease, lack of fresh water, Indian attacks, and hunger all combined to decrease the settler population from 105 to 32.

At this point, Smith took the reins of responsibility. He enforced a work ethic: "He who shall not work, shall not eat." It was strict, but it was effective. The colonists began to look to him as their leader. Smith easily assumed the role. He seemed to be a natural-born leader. His life to this point had been filled with fascinating exploits. In Jamestown, Smith would have his share of adventure.

In December 1607, a group of Indians captured Smith's hunting party. They took Smith to meet their chief,

John Smith

Captain John Smith is a bold and colorful figure in both American myth and history. It is sometimes hard to separate legend from reality in his life.

Smith was born in England in 1580, and he became a soldier at the early age of 16 after his father died. He was a capable and courageous soldier, and his deeds eventually earned him the rank of captain. At one point, he was wounded, captured, and sold into slavery. After he managed to escape, he traveled throughout Russia, Europe, and Africa. When he returned to England, he signed up to sail with the settlers going to Virginia.

One of the most famous episodes of Smith's Jamestown experience involves his relationship with Pocahontas. And here is where myth and reality tend to get blurred. Depending on which version you believe, the tale of Smith and the Indian princess was one of the great love stories of all time, or it may never have happened.

When Smith returned to England, he encouraged more colonization in Virginia. In 1614, he returned to America and explored Maine and Massachusetts Bay. When he retired, he wrote books until he died in 1631. He was 51 years old.

Powhatan. The two men developed a mutual respect.

One legend says that Smith was to be executed by the Indians, but his life was spared when Pocahontas, Powhatan's 11-year-old daughter, intervened on his behalf. Smith would later say that Pocahontas saved his life. However, some believe that Smith and Pocahontas were merely taking part in an Indian ritual, and that Smith's life was never really in danger. Whether or not this story is true, this would not be the only time the young girl helped the colony. Often, Pocahontas would see to it that the Indians gave food to the needy settlers.

After holding Smith captive for a month, the Indians released Smith. When he returned to Jamestown, Smith found that supplies were low and the colonists were fighting with each other.

After dealing with the colonists, Smith went off to explore the Chesapeake Bay region, in search of more supplies. When he came back, the colonists elected him to be the president of their council. Smith took his role and responsibilities very seriously. He enforced strict rules and he instructed the colonists to fortify their defenses. And, using knowledge gained from the Indians, he taught his fellow settlers how to farm. Smith's leadership was a turning point. The weakened settlers not only survived, but the colony started to grow.

In 1609, Smith suffered serious injuries in a gunpowder explosion. He had to go back to England to be treated properly. He would never return to Virginia.

After Smith's departure, Jamestown suffered a horrible period that came to be known as the "starving time" in 1609–10. The colonists were literally starving to death. They were forced to eat anything they could get their hands on, including dogs, cats, mice, and even shoe leather. The population fell from 214 men to 60. The colonists wanted to give up and go home. However, Lord De La Ware, the new governor, arrived with more supplies and convinced them to stay.

In 1612, John Rolfe, an English tobacco businessman, strengthened the colony's economy when he produced a crop of quality tobacco. Tobacco was important to the growth of the southern English colonies. The plant became the first successful *export* from America. In addition, Jamestown enjoyed a period of peace with the Indians when Rolfe married Pocahontas.

Around the same time, Sir Thomas Dale, Jamestown's acting governor, created the "Laws Divine, Morall and Martial" to bring order to the

The first houses built by the earliest Jamestown settlers were topped by thatched roofs. These were made from tree bark and reeds gathered from the James River.

colony. These laws gave rank and responsibility to all of the colonists, including children and women. The laws were very strict and imposed harsh measures on violators. Punishment essentially amounted to physical torture (whippings and painful restraint in *stocks*). Those who broke the law three times were executed.

Dale's laws did create the kind of order that enabled the colony to endure. However, the strictness of the laws discouraged new settlers. The population only began growing again when the laws were eased and the colonists were granted the power of self-government. This led to the creation of the House of Burgesses, the first governmental body in North America. The population grew even more when new settlers were told they'd be able to own their own land. Plantations began to spread outside the Jamestown fort. Jamestown, it appeared, was on its way to becoming a self-sustaining colony.

Unfortunately, not all of the impulses or motives of the Virginia settlers were heroic or noble. In 1619, something happened in Jamestown that would have a profound—and negative—impact on the history of America. That year, the first African slaves came to Jamestown.

As Jamestown grew, settlers started to build farms and plantations along the James River. Tobacco became an important crop. For many people, the amount of money

African slaves arrive at the Jamestown colony, 1619. Slavery provided inexpensive labor for the owners of large tobacco plantations. Although the practice of bringing slaves from Africa to North America was made illegal early in the 19th century, slavery was still permitted in the southern states until after the Civil War ended in 1865.

they made was based on the amount of tobacco they could ship to England. The farmers needed help clearing fields, planting tobacco, taking care of the plants, and harvesting the leaves. The more workers they could afford, the more fields they could cultivate.

At one point, English colonists had tried to make the regional natives work for them. However, they found that the Indians did not make satisfactory workers. The Indians could easily leave and rejoin their people; if they were made captive, they would revolt and kill their captors. The African slave trade provided a simpler alternative.

A Dutch trader brought the first slaves to Jamestown. He exchanged the 20 Africans he had for food. These first slaves, who had been kidnapped from their home-land, became **indentured servants**. That is, they could gain their freedom after working for a certain period of time—usually several years.

Soon, other slavers sailed to Africa. There, they bought kidnapped African natives from their captors. The slaves were brought to America aboard slave ships. The conditions on these ships were terrible. The Africans were kept in chains in overcrowded quarters, which were dirty and disease-ridden. Many of them died at sea.

As Virginia's fledgling tobacco industry began to flourish, laws were passed that legalized slavery. Africans who were brought to North America as slaves would remain slaves for the rest of their lives. Their children would become slaves as well. By the end of the 17th century, several thousand slaves lived in Virginia. By the middle of the 19th century, there would be four million slaves in America.

The Great Massacre of 1622

THE STORY of early English colonization contains many episodes involving *skirmishes* between the Indians and settlers. Much of the time, the colonists and the native inhabitants tried to live together on friendly terms. However, conflicts often arise when two different cultures confront one another. One episode stands out from the rest in terms of bloodshed and brutality.

The Great Massacre of 1622, or the Jamestown Massacre, a surprise attack initiated by a tribal chief, had particularly terrible consequences, both for the settlers and the Native Americans. More than 300 settlers were killed. However, the event extracted a more costly toll on the

Indians. Following the attack, colonists waged a prolonged and methodical assault that wiped out almost all of the Native Americans in the immediate region.

The massacre brought to an end the period of peace and stability that had settled over Jamestown after John Rolfe married Pocahontas. The attack had been planned by Algonquian chief Opechancanough, who was Pocahontas's uncle and Powhatan's brother. It was overwhelming and well-coordinated, involving an alliance of tribes. And it would have been a complete massacre had it not been for Chanco, an Indian boy who had befriended the settlers and alerted Jamestown leaders about the coming attack. As it turned out, Jamestown itself was spared, thanks to the warning, but plantations and settlements along the James River were destroyed and the residents killed.

Ironically, Opechancanough had attended Rolfe's and Pocahontas' wedding ceremony, a celebration that symbolized the goodwill existing between the newcomers and the region's original inhabitants. However, Opechancanough had always hated the "white man." He felt the settlers stole their land and took advantage of the Native Americans.

When Opechancanough became leader of the tribe after Powhatan died in 1618, he found himself in the position to carry out his plan. He convinced other tribes that they could destroy Jamestown and the English settlers with one

Pocahontas

She was born Matoaka around 1595, and when she died in 1617 she was called Lady Rebecca. But everyone knew her as Pocahontas, a name that means "a playful little girl." Pocahontas was the daughter of the chief Powhatan, and she was 11 years old when she first met Captain John Smith and the Jamestown colonists. Although there are many stories about Pocahontas, much of what is remembered about her life might be legend and not fact.

Pocahontas would eventually marry an English tobacco planter named John Rolfe in April 1614. Their union created peace between the settlers and the Indians—a peace that would be shattered by Pocahontas' uncle, Opechancanough, who was responsible for the Great Massacre of 1622.

Pocahontas didn't live long enough to witness the massacre. After her wedding, she went to England with her husband and their son, Thomas. In London, she became a well-known figure and even met King James I. She also met Smith one last time, but the encounter was said to be somewhat strained.

In 1617, Pocahontas prepared to return to Virginia with Rolfe, but before the ship sailed, she became seriously ill and died soon after. She was only 22 years old. Rolfe returned to Virginia. It is believed that he may have been killed during the Great Massacre of 1622.

swift, secret, and massive attack. Then they would be free of the Europeans once and for all, he felt.

The settlers never suspected a thing. The Native Americans pretended to be friendly, even up to the night before the attack, when they had dinner with some of the settlers. In staging the attack, the Indians even used the settlers' boats to transport themselves on the James River.

The Great Massacre of 1622 took place on March 22. The Christian settlers of Jamestown were observing Good Friday. The settlers who lived along the James River were caught completely off guard as they went about their usual business. Some settlers were killed in their fields as they were tending to their crops. Others were killed in their homes when the Native Americans came to their doors pretending to be friendly. Once invited in, the Indians killed and scalped the settlers.

The damage inflicted was swift and devastating, and the savagery was appalling. It took the Indians only a few hours to claim 350 victims—men, women, and children—many of whom were mutilated after being killed. Some outlying settlements were completely destroyed. In other areas, settlers were driven from their homes, which were then burned to the ground.

Jamestown itself was spared the devastation, thanks to Chanco's warning. Chanco told Richard Pace, the

Englishman he lived with, about Opecancanough's plot. Pace rowed down the river to Jamestown and told the governor about the coming attack. The warning allowed those inside Jamestown to prepare. Unfortunately, settlers in outlying areas received no advance warning.

The attack lowered the English population of the region from about 1,400 people to 1,050. However, in the long run, the terrible action proved more disastrous for the Native Americans. Relations between the English settlers and their native neighbors were destroyed. The settlers were hungry for revenge. The fighting became intense at times as the two sides took turns attacking each other.

The settlers' assaults proved to be more effective, however. They launched what amounted to a systematic destruction of the region's native population. For the next 10 years, vengeful Englishmen burned Indian settlements, destroyed their crops, and slaughtered men, women, and children. By 1632, many tribes were completely wiped out. Indians that survived became scattered and they wandered into other regions.

Jamestown had not heard the last of Opechancanough, however, who did not give up so easily. In 1644, he staged another attack on the settlers. This one was less effective. Soon after, an English soldier in Jamestown shot the aging Indian chief in the back.

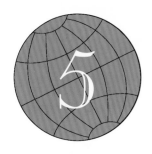

The Pilgrims in Massachusetts

ABOUT THE same time that newly arriving settlers were being given their own land in Jamestown, the Pilgrims were on the way to the New World in a merchant ship named the *Mayflower*. England would soon have its second colony in the New World. And like the Jamestown settlers, the Pilgrims would endure early years of struggle.

The Pilgrims were religious dissenters from England who were **persecuted** for their beliefs. As a group, the Pilgrims disagreed with the Church of England, the official religion of their home country. The Pilgrims wanted to break away from the church, and saw the New World as a place where they could worship as they wished. So, while Jamestown

The Pilgrims named their colony Plymouth, after the harbor in England from which the *Mayflower* had sailed.

was set up essentially as a merchant enterprise, the Pilgrims' colony at Plymouth was founded on philosophical and spiritual beliefs.

The Pilgrim experience greatly influenced the creation of other colonies and the birth of the United States. In establishing their colony, the Pilgrims promoted the idea of people governing themselves. They embraced values that would become firmly ingrained in the character of an emerging nation.

The inspiring story of the Plymouth colony began in 1620, when 101 Pilgrims boarded the *Mayflower* to make a 11-week voyage across the rough seas of the North Atlantic. A man named William Bradford was the leader of the group. Their military leader was Miles Standish, a soldier who had met the Pilgrims a few years earlier when they were living in *exile* in Holland. The captain of the *Mayflower* was Christopher Jones.

The journey was cramped and uncomfortable. The only food was cold biscuits, cheese, and salted meat or fish. Some

Although no authentic plans of the *Mayflower* are known to exist, the ship was probably like other merchant vessels of the time. Historians believe it was about 100 feet long, 26 feet wide, and had three masts.

of the passengers developed a disease called *scurvy*, which was common on long sea voyages. However, only one person died on board the *Mayflower*.

While at sea, the Pilgrims drew up the Mayflower Compact, one of the most important documents in American history. The Compact formed the foundation of the Pilgrims' government. It stated that the Pilgrims would create their own laws and choose their own leaders. Among its democratic principles were the concepts of equal justice and majority rule.

In November 1620, the *Mayflower* landed on Cape Cod in an area now known as Massachusetts. The Pilgrims had wanted to land much farther south, but storms at sea had blown their ship off course. At first, the area they explored looked bleak and inhospitable. It was full of sandy beaches, high dunes, and tall grass. Undaunted, the Pilgrims sailed along the coast, looking for a more suitable location to establish a colony. Finally, on December 21, they found a spot where fresh water was available.

Soon the Pilgrims were hard at work carving out a site

Two boys were born on the *Mayflower* during the Pilgrims trip to the New World. The first, Oceanus Hopkins, was born at sea. The second, Peregrine White, was born as the ship was anchored off the coast of Cape Cod.

The leader of the Pilgrims, William Bradford, is seated at a table while reading the Mayflower Compact on board their ship. Bradford (1590–1657) was governor of the Plymouth colony from 1621 until his death, except for five years during which he refused election. Much of what we know about life in the colony comes from his book *History of Plymouth Plantation*, a chronicle of events from 1620 to 1646.

and building shelters against the cruel northern climate. However, the Pilgrims were weak and hungry, and their first winter in the New World was a hard one. They had little food. Starvation and disease killed nearly half of them. This time would become known as the "Great Sickness."

By March, the survivors had managed to build a small community comprised of private shelters and a common house. They also began planting crops.

A crucial and historic episode occurred on March 16,

1621, when an English-speaking Native American named Samoset ventured into their camp and made friends with the settlers. The next day, Samoset returned with Squanto, another English-speaking native. Squanto would play an important role in the Pilgrims' survival.

Squanto had traveled much during his interesting life. He had crossed the Atlantic several times, lived in England for a while, and had sailed with Captain John Smith on his last voyage back to the New World. Squanto was originally a member of the Pawtuxet tribe, and his real name was Tisquantum. He had learned to speak English through his association with Europeans during his travels.

The Pilgrims made their two visitors feel welcome. Soon, Squanto taught his new friends how to fish and plant crops, such as corn, beans, and pumpkins. He also taught them skills that would be essential to their survival, such as how to find clams, how to hunt for wild game, and how to construct houses that would provide suitable shelter against the elements.

Squanto also helped the Pilgrims establish a peace treaty with the local Wampanoag tribe and their leader, Chief Massasoit. The relationship proved to be good for both sides. Settlers and Indians learned from each other and shared food. This led to a three-day celebration that has been called the first American Thanksgiving. It took place

Miles Standish

He was called the "Hero of New England" and he was among the first Pilgrims to step off the *Mayflower*. Brave, tough, and hot-tempered, Miles Standish was the kind of man you would want on your side in a fight.

Born in Lancashire, England, Standish became a soldier. Early in his career, he served in the Netherlands and met the people who would become the American Pilgrims. He sailed with the Pilgrims on the Mayflower and became the military leader of Plymouth Colony.

Quick to anger and quick to act, Standish defended the colony against Indian attacks several times. When he was called on to protect the people living in the town of Weymouth, he killed Pecksuot, a tribal chief, with the leader's own knife.

In 1631, Standish settled in Duxbury, a town he helped found in Massachusetts, where he became assistant magistrate. He died in his home in 1656.

in October 1621 after the harvest, when the Pilgrims and the Wampanoags shared their bounties. The menu included food that the two groups had grown or hunted. The first Thanksgiving table was filled with deer meat, duck, goose, turkey, clams, eels, corn, dried berries, pumpkins, and wine.

Things appeared to be looking up for the Pilgrims. They had forged a peaceful alliance with the local tribe, built up their settlement, and were amassing a store of food.

Unfortunately, the optimism that came with the first Thanksgiving was short-lived. After the feast, the Pilgrims realized they had overestimated their harvest. Worried that they wouldn't have enough food to last the winter, they began *rationing* food. The situation worsened with the arrival of more settlers, who came to Plymouth with few supplies. The threat of starvation loomed once again.

The Pilgrims made it through the winter, but their food was gone by the spring of 1622. And, with the local wildlife population diminishing, the desperate settlers were pinning all their hopes on that year's harvest.

Even though the harvest that fall was not as good as the Pilgrims had hoped, the colony was able to survive. It received much-needed aid when *Discovery*, a ship sailing from Jamestown to England, made a stop at Plymouth. The ship's captain provided the Pilgrims with items they could trade to the Indians for food.

Finally, fortune smiled on the Pilgrims. The harvest of 1623 was a good one. Soon after, more settlers arrived. The favorable reversal of fortune was long-lasting. The Pilgrims never went hungry again, and for the next few years the Plymouth colony flourished.

A KEY into the

LANGUAGE

OF

AMERICA:

OR,

An help to the *Language* of the *Natives*
in that part of AMERICA, called
NEW-ENGLAND.

Together, with briefe *Observations* of the Cu-
stomes, Manners and Worships, &c. of the
aforesaid *Natives*, in Peace and Warre,
in Life and Death.

On all which are added Spirituall *Observations*,
Generall and Particular by the *Authour*, of
chiefe and speciall use (upon all occasions,) to
all the *English* Inhabiting those parts ;
yet pleasant and profitable to
the view of all men :

BY ROGER WILLIAMS
of *Providence* in *New-England.*

LONDON,
Printed by *Gregory Dexter*, 1643.

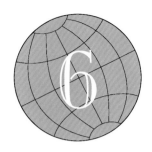

The Puritans in Massachusetts

NOT LONG after the Pilgrims gained a strong foothold in Plymouth, the Puritans began leaving England to come to the New World. The Puritan emigration to North American shores represented a large and rapid increase in the settler population. In 1630, 1,000 Puritans landed in Massachusetts Bay. A few months later, 500 more followed. By 1640, there were 20,000 Puritans in the Massachusetts area. Like the Pilgrims before them, these new colonists were hardworking and industrious. They made their living by farming, fishing, and building ships. In only 10 years, they had spread out from the first settlement in Boston and established a thriving community. The Puritans were also responsible for establishing new colonies in Connecticut, Rhode Island, and New Hampshire.

Sometimes, people tend to think of the Pilgrims and the Puritans as one and the same. This is not correct. True, Pilgrims and Puritans both led disciplined lives, were very religious, and believed in a strong work ethic, but there was a major difference between the two groups. The Pilgrims wanted to separate themselves from the Church of England, while the Puritans only wanted to reform, or "purify," the church. That is how the Puritans got their name. Still, the Puritans, like the Pilgrims, wanted religious freedom. They came to America because the king of England, Charles I, opposed their attempt to reform the Church of England.

In 1629, before leaving for the New World, the Puritans obtained a royal charter from King Charles, who was happy to see them go. This document, called the Charter of the Company of Massachusetts Bay in New England, became the constitution of the Massachusetts Bay Colony. It gave the Puritans the right to govern themselves. Like the Mayflower Compact, the charter is one of the most important documents in early American history.

A year later, the Puritans left England for Massachusetts Bay with 11 ships. John Winthrop, the Puritans' elected leader, helped pay for the trip, and he would use his own money to help feed some of the colonists when they became hungry. Like colonists before them, the Puritans suffered through their first winter. Two hundred members died during the winter, and 200 more returned to England in the spring.

Even though Puritan leaders spoke out publicly against the form of government called "democracy," the Puritans integrated democratic principles into their own government. Each taxpayer had an equal say in creation of the laws. However, the Puritans felt that government and religion should be closely connected, so church officials governed the people. They felt that civil laws should be designed to reflect God's laws. This was called the "Puritan

John Winthrop (1588–1649) was the first governor of the Massachusetts Bay Colony. Winthrop founded the city of Boston, which became the center of the colony. He devoted most of his life to the success of the Massachusetts Bay Colony. Except for brief intervals he served as its governor until his death.

One of the most important Puritan leaders was clergyman Cotton Mather (1663–1728). His father, Increase Mather, was a Puritan preacher who played an important part in the Salem witchcraft trials. They preached together at Boston's North Church until Increase's death in 1721. Cotton Mather was interested in science as well as religion, and wrote more than 400 books. However, he also tried to enforce strict Puritan traditions on the congregation.

Plan." Puritans believed God had one perfect plan, and they tried to live their lives by this plan. And, because they believed God controlled their government, the Puritans allowed the government to exercise great control over their daily lives.

The day started early for the Puritans. Children did chores and attended school, while the adults tended to the farming and household duties. The day ended early, too. Puritan families would often go to bed after eating their evening supper.

The Puritans subjected themselves to many rules. Citizens were not allowed to wear fancy clothing, and women had to keep their hair cut short. It was forbidden for anyone to play cards, make music, or dance. Holidays were not celebrated, and religious wedding ceremonies were forbidden, too.

The most important rules, however, involved church. The Puritan Sabbath began

> **The Puritans founded Harvard University, one of the most famous colleges in the United States, in 1636. However, the school did not open for instruction until 1638. That year, Harvard had nine students and one instructor.**

Saturday evening and lasted all day Sunday. On Sunday, the Puritans spent the whole day in church, taking only one break for lunch. During the Sabbath, people were not allowed to work, play, or visit with friends and neighbors.

Puritan leaders did not tolerate individualism very well. Nor did they tolerate opposing religious beliefs. As might be expected, such restrictions produced *dissent*. Some Puritans began embracing different ideas, and they were not afraid to express them. The most outspoken dissenters included Roger Williams, Anne Hutchinson, and Thomas Hooker.

Puritan leaders did not like it when anyone spoke out against the government. They *banished* those who spoke out, meaning that the dissenters were forced to leave the colony. This led to the creation of new settlements. When Roger Williams was banished for advocating the separation

The northernmost American colonies—Massachusetts, Rhode Island, Connecticut, and New Hampshire—were called New England. This was a name given by John Smith when he explored the area in 1614. Today, New England also includes the states of Maine and Vermont.

of church and government, he founded a colony in Providence, Rhode Island. The colony was originally intended as a place for other Puritan dissenters and it attracted many of the disenchanted.

Hutchinson also publicly disagreed with the Puritan leaders. She invited fellow dissenters into her home, where she offered Bible studies and expressed to them a concept of spiritual individualism. John Winthrop was angered that a woman would act this way, and he brought charges against Hutchinson. She, too, was banished and went to Rhode Island. Hooker, who publicly disagreed with Winthrop and Richard Mather, another Puritan leader, took 800 people with him and founded a colony in Hartford, Connecticut.

Today, many of the Puritans' rules and laws may seem rigid and old-fashioned. But the impact this group of people had on America is undeniable. The Puritans were resourceful, productive, and responsible. They possessed high values and ideals. These ideals, and other views and attitudes of English colonists in North America, became an integral part of the American character.

By the end of the 17th century, English colonies had been established along the Atlantic coast of North America, including Maryland (established 1634), Connecticut (1635), Rhode Island (1636), Carolina (1663; it would be divided into North and South Carolina in 1730), New Hampshire (1679), and Pennsylvania (1682). A colony would be established in New Jersey in 1702, and in Georgia in 1732. In addition, the English would take over the Dutch colony of New Netherlands, which they renamed New York, as well as a Swedish colony in Delaware.

The promise of the New World was not limited to the English, however. Immigrants to North America included Germans, Irish, Poles, Scots, Jews, Dutch, French, Italians, and other nationalities. These people hoped to make a new life for themselves in the underpopulated colonies.

The work of the earliest English explorers and coloniz-ers of North America made these colonies possible. And one day the 13 American colonies would unite in a war against an unjust king, and declare themselves a new nation—the United States of America.

Chronology

1492 Christopher Columbus lands in America.

1497 John Cabot, sailing in the service of England, explores the coast of North America in search of the northwest passage.

1583 English explorer Sir Humphrey Gilbert tries and fails to establish an English colony in Newfoundland.

1584 Sir Walter Raleigh is issued a charter to explore and colonize the New World; during the next six years he sends out four voyages. Two attempts to colonize Roanoke Island fail; the second attempt, in 1587, results in the disappearance of all the settlers.

1590 On August 18, John White lands on Roanoke Island and begins a search for the lost colonists; among the missing are White's daughter, son-in-law and granddaughter.

1606 King James I grants the Virginia Company a charter to start a colony in Virginia; on December 20, a group of settlers leave England for Virginia.

1607 Captain John Smith and the other settlers arrive in Virginia on May 14; they immediately set to work building a colony that they name Jamestown.

1609 Jamestown settlers endure the "starving time." More than one-third of the colonists die during the winter.

1612 The Jamestown settlers begin to cultivate tobacco, which will become an important moneymaking crop.

Chronology

1614 John Rolfe marries Pocahontas, beginning a period of peace between Jamestown and the Powhatan Indians.

1617 Pocahontas dies in England at age 22.

1618 Powhatan dies, allowing Opechancanough to assume leadership of the Powhatan tribe; on October 29, Sir Walter Raleigh is executed.

1619 The first African slaves arrive in Jamestown.

1620 In September, the Pilgrims leave England for North America in the merchant ship *Mayflower*; in November, the ship lands on Cape Cod; on December 21, the Pilgrims disembark at Plymouth and establish a colony.

1621 In March, the Pilgrims meet Squanto, an English-speaking Indian who will be instrumental in their survival; in mid-October, the Pilgrims and the Wampanoag tribe come together for a Thanksgiving feast.

1622 On March 22, Good Friday, Opechancanough leads a devastating attack on settlers living near Jamestown.

1629 King Charles of England grants a charter to the Puritans, who want to leave England.

1630 The Puritans leave England and land in Massachusetts, where they establish the Massachusetts Bay Colony.

1631 Captain John Smith dies in England at 51.

Glossary

armada—a fleet of warships.

artisan—a person who practices a particular craft.

banish—to send somebody to another place as a punishment.

barrier reef—a coral reef that runs along a shore and is separated from it by a lagoon.

cartographer—a person who makes maps.

charter—a special privilege or authority granted to a particular person or group.

chasm—a marked division, separation, or difference.

dissent—to refuse to conform to the authority, doctrines, and practices of an established church.

emigrant—a person who leaves his or her place of residence or country to live elsewhere.

exile—an unwilling absence from a home country because of religious or political reasons.

export—a commodity taken from one country to another for purposes of trade.

fortification—a structure, such as a wall, that is built in order to strengthen a place's defenses.

hurricane—a severe tropical storm with heavy rain and strong winds.

Glossary

indentured servant—a person who is bound to a term of service for a set period of time (often seven years).

northwest passage—a route that explorers of the 15th, 16th, and 17th centuries believed existed through the continent of North America, connecting the Atlantic Ocean to the Pacific; this route would enable ships from Europe to reach Asia and India by sailing west.

persecute—to cause someone to suffer because of his or her beliefs.

ration—to distribute sparingly, such as food or water, to conserve supplies.

scurvy—a disease that was common on long journeys, caused by a lack of vitamin C. Symptoms include spongy gums and loose teeth, soreness in the arm and leg joints, and bleeding into the skin and mucous membranes.

skirmish—a minor fight.

stocks—a wooden frame in which criminals were secured by the hands and/or feet and left in public to be ridiculed or abused.

Further Reading

Hakim, Joy. *A History of Us: Making Thirteen Colonies*. New York: Oxford University Press, 1999.

Mancall, Peter C. *Envisioning America: English Plans for the Colonization of North America, 1580–1640*. Boston: Bedford Books, 1995.

Quinn, Arthur. *A New World: An Epic of Colonial America from the Founding of Jamestown to the Fall of Quebec*. Boston: Faber & Faber, 1994.

Quinn, David B. *England and the Discovery of America, 1481–1620*. New York: Knopf, 1974.

Sakurai, Gail. *The Jamestown Colony*. Danbury: Children's Press, 1997.

Internet Resources

Jamestown

http://jefferson.village.virginia.edu/vcdh/jamestown/

http://www.nps.gov/colo/

http://www.apva.org/jr.html

http://www.iath.virginia.edu/vcdh/jamestown/

The Pilgrims and Plymouth Colony

http://www.rootsweb.com/~mosmd/

http://www.plimoth.org/Library/pilgrim.htm

The Puritans and Massachusetts Bay Colony

http://lonestar.texas.net/~mseifert/puritan.html

http://xroads.virginia.edu/~CAP/puritan/purhist.html

Index

Photo Credits

Front cover: National Park Service, Colonial National Historical Park
Back cover: Mary Evans Picture Library; The Library of Virginia; National Park Service, Colonial National Historical Park

About the Author

Dan Harvey is a freelance journalist whose work has earned him three national journalism awards and three Pennsylvania journalism awards. During his career, he has been a sports writer and editor, a newspaper editor, and the managing editor of a medical magazine. He currently produces study guides, magazine articles, and book manuscripts. He lives in Wilmington, Delaware, with his wife, Monica.